MONEY HAPPINE$$:™
FIVE WEALTH LESSONS WITH
PROFESSOR OCEAN™

JIM EXLEY, PhD, PATRICK DOYLE, PhD
& W. KEITH CAMPBELL, PhD

For more information:
ProfessorOCEAN@Professor-OCEAN.com

731 Duval Station Road #107 #283
Jacksonville,
FL 32218

ISBN 979-8-218-21310-7

MONEY
HAPPINE$$:™
FIVE WEALTH LESSONS WITH
PROFESSOR
OCEAN™

JIM EXLEY, PhD, PATRICK DOYLE, PhD
& W. KEITH CAMPBELL, PhD

WELCOME BACK

Welcome back to the world of Professor OCEAN!

In this edition, we explore the world of money and finance. However, this is not a budgeting or financial planning book. After all, we're psych professors! This is a book on how to think about money from a psychological perspective. You are a one-of-a-kind work of art with unique traits, experiences, and stories that make up your personality. Building on our first book, you will learn how your personality—using the OCEAN model of personality—affects the way you handle money.

We will quickly revisit the Big Five traits:

Openness
Conscientiousness
Extraversion
Agreeableness
Neuroticism

More importantly, we will introduce you to

the concept of Money Happiness. Like it or not, research shows that how we feel about money has a massive impact on how we feel about our lives.[1] Therefore, we might as well measure Money Happiness and attempt to improve it as much as possible.

As a business fable, this book is meant to convey large amounts of information in a short period of time—possibly even one sitting. Like the first book, this book is written in layers. However, this time, the layers include finance and psychology. Whether you are just here for the story or you are an experienced researcher from academia, there is something in the book for everyone. We also understand that this new framework may be controversial. The concepts may challenge your traditional thinking, and you may feel yourself pushing back. If so, we remind you that's what we intended to do! As our world increases in complexity, our "numeracy," which is our ability to think quickly and accurately about money, should adapt too!

Thankfully, Professor OCEAN's got some wisdom to share!

BACKGROUND

The old psych professor, Professor OCEAN, has been back on campus for a few years now. After a distinguished research and teaching career at the university, he took multiple assignments around the globe (in great surfing spots of course!) and started and sold a company along the way. His current auditorium seminar class is standing room only, and he often takes time to coach students and members of the community upon request—as long as they buy him coffee from Roy's across from his park bench and occasionally bring Sigmund, his loyal canine sidekick, a puppy treat.

$

CHAPTER
One

INTRODUCTION TO MONEY HAPPINESS

On a cool, spring morning, Professor OCEAN was sitting on his campus park bench near the school monument drinking his shot-in-the-dark coffee, reading the morning narrative, and talking to Sigmund, his loyal canine sidekick. The old campus quad was popping with spring leaves and flowers. The pear trees offered a pungent smell, and the school beautification crew (also known as the School of Landscape Architecture) was putting the finishing touches on their daily perfecting of the grounds, giving the quad the look of a certain type of academic utopia. The chipmunks were playing hide and seek around the grand oak tree. Constantine, a former student of Professor OCEAN and the football team's gargantuan 6'9" starting left tackle, walked by dressed in team-issued clothes with matching backpack.

"Good morning, Constantine!" Professor OCEAN called out.

"Morning, Coach," Constantine replied, using the moniker he had for all his elders.

Professor OCEAN paused, noticing a slight difference in the mood of his former student.

"What's going on, Constantine? You're usually on top of the world."

"Nobody sitting on your park bench with you today, Coach?" Constantine replied, clearly avoiding the question.

Professor OCEAN looked to the companion barking and wagging beside him. "Well, I was giving Sigmund a little coaching."

At that, Constantine laughed. "Trouble at the dog park again?"

"Yep, it seems Sigmund has a 'heavyweight' heart stuffed inside of a 'lightweight' body. He keeps wanting to show James's German Shepard who's boss. Usually, my thought is that experience is the best teacher, but I'm too old and soft to let Sigmund learn that lesson the hard way. So, we're just doing a little talk therapy to work it out."

Constantine laughed again and questioned if this approach actually worked on dogs.

"Of course not!" Professor OCEAN replied with a grin. "But it makes me feel better."

The two men paused, letting the silence sit between them for a moment. Finally, Professor OCEAN spoke up.

"Well, enough about my problems," the old man said. "What's up with you?"

Constantine considered his options for a moment. He could avoid the conversation, but he knew the old man well enough to know he would keep asking until Constantine started talking. So, he gave in.

"Well, you know about those new name, image, and likeness deals, right?" Constantine began. "Sometimes they shorten it to NIL, but it basically means student athletes like me can get paid to be in commercials and stuff like that. Well, I just signed one of those deals with a local business."

At this, Professor OCEAN perked up. "That's

incredible, Constantine! I can't think of a more deserving athlete on this campus. You've worked hard in the classroom, volunteered in the community, and kept your nose clean. Not to mention you're pretty decent at football! I have to wonder what the problem is here."

Constantine sighed. "It's the money, Coach. I think they might have paid me too much."

Too much? Professor OCEAN sat stunned in silence at the thought this could even be possible!

"When I was in high school, I worked hard during the summer. Mowed lawns, delivered pizzas, walked dogs—you name it," Constantine continued. "I've never had more than $5,000 in my checking account and that was only for a short time before I used $4,000 of it to buy my car."

"My guess is that if you are smart with your money, Constantine, you'll never have only a thousand bucks in your checking account for the rest of your life," the Professor reassured him.

At this, Constantine sighed. "That's the problem. I don't even know what it means to be 'smart with my money.' You see, Coach, I never learned any personal finance in any of my classes. My parents taught me a lot, but personal finance wasn't their specialty either. Now, they know I've signed the deal. All my teammates know, too. It's already been in the media. Coach Russell was so proud he wanted everybody to know. Guess the school thinks it will help recruiting if their players are getting paid. The point is, it's a lot of money . . . and a lot of pressure. My guess is that the amount this business is about to drop into my checking account is more than my parents have in their retirement account!"

Professor OCEAN nodded, listening as Constantine continued to share his newfound financial success and the subsequent worries that came with it.

"That's not even all of it! In addition to practice, school, and volunteering, now I've got folks wanting to talk to me about money. My coaches are worried I'm going to get in trouble with it, my teammates want me to take them out to dinner and bankroll their parties, and financial planners are calling me wanting to help me manage it. These planners are supposed to be making it easier on me, but I can't understand all the big financial words they use. Yesterday, my job was to be the best player I could be, and today, it feels like I'm running a business with no training."

"You should have signed up for the new 'Wealth Science' class I'm teaching through the psych department," Professor OCEAN told him.

Constantine knew about the class the Professor mentioned. He wanted to take it, in fact, but the class was taught too late in the day and conflicted with his practice schedule. "So, when does the money hit your account?" Professor OCEAN asked.

"Well, the bulk of it hits six weeks from today, but they gave me $1,000 up front," Constantine said, pausing for a moment before finally continuing. "If I'm being honest, Professor, it's already gone."

"Gone?!"

"Gone, Coach. I didn't really need it right now, and it wasn't doing much good sitting in my savings account. Some of the guys around the dorm talked me into buying some cryptos and startup tech stocks."

Professor OCEAN understood, "Those things have been hot lately." Of course this young athlete would invest his first funds there!

"Well, I must have bought the cold ones because my digital wallet says I've now got $100," Constantine continued, clearly defeated. "If this is what investing is like, I don't think I'm built for it. I don't even have the heart to tell my mom it's already gone."

Suddenly, the Professor perked up. A smile spread across his face as he leaned toward Constantine and slapped him on the back. "This is great news, Constantine!"

Clearly shocked, Constantine looked at the Professor with wide eyes. "Great news? What are you talking about?"

"Well, you paid a small price to learn that money can bring pain as well as pleasure. That is why my focus is always on Money Happiness first and foremost! In my consulting work, I've met some blissfully happy people with very little and more than my share of miserable multimillionaires, too. To get to the place of

Money Happiness, I've boiled it down to five key money lessons. The good news for you? I can teach them all from this very park bench."

"Money Happiness?" Constantine asked. "What is that?"

At this question, Professor OCEAN beamed. He was ready to teach.

"Simple definition really," he began. "Money Happiness is the feeling that your financial life is going well, not poorly. If we are going to feel something about money—and we all know that money generates a lot of emotion—we might as well be honest about it, measure it, and figure out what boosts it."

Constantine listened closely, taking it all in. He'd never thought about it that way.

"On a scale of 0–10, with 0 being you're not sleeping at night and 10 being you're feeling the best you've ever felt in your life, where are you right now as it relates to your feelings about money?" the Professor asked.

For a moment, Constantine considered the question. After a long pause, he finally answered. "I'm probably at a 4, Coach."

"Wow!" Professor OCEAN exclaimed in

reply. "You just signed the biggest contract of your life, but the way you feel is a failing grade! Sounds like we have some work to do! Plus, six weeks gives us just enough time for my five lessons on money before the rest of yours comes in."

Constantine chuckled at the old man's enthusiasm. Leave it to him to find the silver lining!

"The lessons are the same that I teach students who will be getting their first jobs in a few months, but it will be fun to go through the athlete's version with you. So, what do you say? Thursdays at 7:00 am before your first class?"

"Same as the last time we met together, huh? Is the price the same as the last time, too?"

The Professor nodded enthusiastically. All his former students knew the price of admission: one of Roy's large black coffees with an added shot of espresso.

"One other question," Constantine said. "Can my girlfriend, Charlotte, come, too? She's the captain of the soccer team and just signed a larger deal than me. Plus, she let a friend of the family invest her money in his startup business.

She's concerned she'll never see it again."

"The more the merrier!" the Professor agreed.

Relieved to have a plan to get himself on track, Constantine stood. He would be ready on Thursday for the first lesson and even more so with Charlotte in tow.

As he turned to leave, Constantine asked the Professor one final question. "Coach, how come I'm a senior in college and no one has ever taught me about money before?"

A mystic spark lit in the Professor's piercing blue eyes. "Now that's a big question, isn't it? Let's leave that one for later. For now, I'll just say it's the main reason I'm still hanging around this place!"

Taking the answer for now, Constantine thanked Professor OCEAN for his time and scurried away, eager to tell Charlotte about the plan he'd set up for them both.

As he left, Sigmund barked and wagged his approval. Even the dog was excited to spend more time with his old friend on the park bench. Plus, he knew he could count on Charlotte to bring the dog treats!

Being "smart" with money is not as hard as it seems. However, Constantine had to admit to Professor OCEAN—and himself—that he needed to think differently. By agreeing to another lesson on the park bench, Constantine opened himself up to a new way of thinking. Now, the question is: Are you open to the same?

How do you think about money? How could you think about money differently now that you have learned about Money Happiness?

$

CHAPTER
Two

LESSON ONE:
OCEAN PERSONALITY TRAITS
AND MONEY

As the clock hit 6:30 am that next Thursday, Constantine was already standing at the counter of Roy's waiting on three large coffees with added shots. It was so early that only he and Roy were in the café, so his coffees were getting Roy's special treatment. Last time Constantine sat on the bench with Professor OCEAN, he figured he'd give the old man's coffee concoction a try, and as it turned out, he liked it! He'd been drinking it ever since. Of course, a $5.00 coffee didn't fit an athlete's budget on a regular basis, but Constantine was hoping his NIL deal was about to change all that.

"Let me guess," Roy said, handing the coffees to Constantine across the counter. "Another round with Professor O on the park bench?"

"How'd you guess?" Constantine replied with a smile.

"Been there a few times myself! So, you guys gonna win it all this year?"

"That's the plan!"

"I hope you're able to do it! You guys will be legends if you can pull it off! Heck, I might be willing to offer free coffees for life to all championship team members! Plus, it would be great to hear that stadium roar like the old days. Good for business!"

Constantine stuck his hand out. "I'll make that deal right now! Shake on it?"

Roy took the athlete's hand, shocked by the sheer size of the left tackle's bear paw, and shook on the hopeful championship.

As Constantine exited the coffee shop, he found Charlotte waiting for him outside. Together, they rounded the corner with three coffees and a pup cup to find Professor OCEAN, green alligator belt and all, with Sigmund and his matching green collar sitting alertly by his side.

"Early as always!" the Professor greeted them. "Good morning! Good to see you both!"

Together, the three of them settled on the park bench with their coffees in hand.

"So, you two want to 'Forrest Gump' your finances?" the Professor asked.

"Forrest Gump?" Charlotte replied, clearly confused.

"Remember when Lieutenant Dan told Forrest he didn't have to worry about money 'no more'?" Constantine explained, clearly catching the Professor's drift. "Forrest said, 'That's good, one less thing!' Well, Professor OCEAN is our Lieutenant Dan! Regardless of how much I make from football or you make from soccer, we don't want to worry about money anymore, and he can help us with that."

"Well said, Constantine!" Professor OCEAN encouraged. "You're always the thoughtful one, aren't you? That's what I love about you. It's why I know you will be a huge success with money, with a little coaching of course!"

At this, Constantine was intrigued. "How's that, Coach?"

"Well, you remember your OCEAN traits from our last sessions, right?"

"Of course! You said personality touches everything. It's something I think about every day!"

"Great! So, what was your highest scoring trait?"

"C for conscientiousness! You called it my cardinal trait and said I had to be careful not to be obsessive about stuff."

"That's the potential negative of the trait, yes, but the potential positive of high C is that it's known as the wealth trait."[2]

Constantine sat silently for a moment as the information sunk in.

"Your personality can be your greatest strength or weakness, even as it relates to money," the Professor affirmed.

Constantine wasn't sure what the old man meant by this. So, he asked him to explain.

"Well, remember last time when we worked on your high C? We said it was great for showing up on time, working hard, and preparing," the Professor explained, jogging his student's memory, "but, in games, it was leading to over thinking and analysis paralysis, right?"

"That's right," Constantine remembered.

"Money, like most things in life, is the same way. Your unique personality will determine the unique money path that is right for you. It might not work for others, but who cares? It's your path!"

"So, I'm guessing we aren't going to talk about money today. We're back to psychology and personality?"

"Right again! Under pressure—which six weeks to learn certainly is—a person always reverts to the level of their training. Even though we're talking about money, I'm still an old psych professor at heart!"

Charlotte, who was listening intently at the exchange between the two men, finally broke into the conversation. "Wait, I think I'm a little behind here? Personality psychology?"

"You remember when I met with Professor OCEAN last time, and he taught me the OCEAN stuff?" Constantine asked, looking on as Charlotte nodded.

"Of course! I just never took the test, so I'm not exactly sure what my personality is."

Smiling, Constantine proudly exclaimed, "Well I know! High O, high C, moderate E, high A, and moderate N!"

"What does all that stand for?" Charlotte asked, eager to learn more.

Here, the Professor cut in. "The first thing to know is each person has each of the five traits. Each of them exists on a scale from low to high. Each person has a given amount of each trait, and they all work together; it's just a matter of how much or how little."

"Got it!" Charlotte confirmed.

"Constantine, why don't you bring Charlotte up to speed on each trait?" the Professor said, giving the reins to his former student.

"Well, O is for openness. A high level of openness means you are open to new ideas, like the new tattoo on your ankle," Constantine explained. "C is for conscientiousness. You know the way you are a little OCD like me? Everything has to be done perfectly or it drives you crazy, right?"

At this, Charlotte nodded in agreement.

"That's your C!" Constantine continued. "E stands for extraversion. Yours is moderately high, as you are a leader, so you have the drive and assertiveness side of extraversion, but you don't necessarily love lots of socializing or public speaking. A stands for agreeableness, and yours is really high. You may be the nicest person I've ever met!"

Charlotte was touched at both the compliment and her boyfriend's awareness of who she was.

"And finally, N is for neuroticism, or emotionality," he continued. "You are a bit sensitive to threats and risk, which makes you great at defense and protecting the goal. Also, you can be fairly emotional at times. Remember last week during the game when the wing didn't do what she was supposed to do?"

"I lit her up!" Charlotte exclaimed with pride.

"Yeah, you did! She needed it, too! That's your emotionality on display. You also worry and sometimes get sad or down on yourself a bit, which is also rooted in neuroticism."

Finally, the Professor cut in. "Great description, Constantine. I couldn't have said it better myself!"

Surprised, Charlotte couldn't believe her boyfriend could pinpoint her personality so specifically and so quickly. Professor OCEAN must've been a good teacher.

"But what does all this have to do with money?" Charlotte finally asked.

"Well, here's the thing," Professor OCEAN began, "personality relates to *everything*! But what we have recently found is that the OCEAN traits also correlate with various money behaviors."

"That's really interesting," Charlotte replied, considering the Professor's words.

"Yep! Interesting indeed!" Professor OCEAN confirmed. "OCEAN tells us a lot about money behaviors. For example, high Os typically like to learn and try new things but don't always turn that into better results. On the other hand, high Es make bigger incomes and like risk but are not as financially literate, which creates interesting results!"

Constantine let out a frustrated laugh. "Sounds like the dude who told me to buy crypto!"

"This stuff does work that way," Professor OCEAN replied. "Interestingly, a high E won't always convert their high income and risk taking into better overall results."

Charlotte nodded, really getting it. "That makes sense. Ready, fire, aim, huh?"

"That's right! Now, high Cs do like to learn and also make high incomes but don't like risk all that much. However, through their hard work and discipline, they often have a higher net worth than others, which is the value of all their assets less their liabilities. Of course, they could make it a bit easier on themselves by taking a little more risk."

"Sounds similar to my football practicing and playing!" Constantine exclaimed.

"Similar indeed! Moving on, high As, despite being really pleasant to be around, don't like risk all that much and have a hard time converting their skills into higher incomes and net worth."

"So nice girls and guys really do finish last when it comes to money?" Charlotte asked, a little discouragement showing in her voice.

"Maybe! Very astute observation, Charlotte!" the Professor credited her. "Researchers have used that very expression to describe the financial downsides of agreeableness.[3] But yes, research does show high As tend to make less money and take less risk, which is not a great combination when it comes to money."

"That leaves N," Constantine said, "which I'm guessing is not good for money."

"Well, high Ns are great at detecting possible threats," the Professor said, "but sometimes they're a bit too sensitive and avoid risk, which makes it hard to put their money to work."

Charlotte was on the edge of her seat. Or rather, the edge of her bench! "Wow! This stuff is fascinating! This makes me want to go back and take the test to see where I am."

Professor OCEAN nodded in agreement. "You should! OCEAN offers significant clues into who you are."

"Don't forget the rest, Coach," Constantine urged. "You've gotta know who you are in order to figure out what you want and how you're gonna get it, right?"[4]

At this, Charlotte looked puzzled.

"He's referencing my three rules," the Professor explained. "Or rather, my three questions: 1) Who am I? 2) What do I want? 3) What is my plan for getting it?"

"Oh, I like it," Charlotte said. "Sounds like I should have been on this bench back when I was a freshman!"

Seeing her intrigue, Constantine playfully elbowed Charlotte. "I told you!"

"No worries," Professor OCEAN encouraged, "you're here now, and there is plenty of time!"

"So, how do we use OCEAN to understand money?" Constantine asked, trying to return the Professor to the lesson at hand.

"That's another lesson for another time. Let's just suffice it to say that one-size-fits-all money advice works about as well as one-size-fits-all football and soccer coaching."

Charlotte broke in again. "This stuff is amazing. I'm sitting here thinking about my teammates' personalities and how all this makes sense. Also, isn't the all-American pass rusher the one who told us to buy the cryptos? He seemed so confident."

At this, Constantine groaned. "Ugh, don't bring that up. 'Often wrong never in doubt'— that's what we say about Azil."

"That actually makes sense," the Professor cut in to explain. "A great team needs all types. And of course, certain positions need more aggression. For example, high Es don't just operate that way on the field; they tend to operate that way in life, including with money."

"How so?" Charlotte asked, imploring the Professor to continue.

"Based on our personalities, each of us has different strengths, weaknesses, and dislikes when it comes to money. This causes each of us to think a little differently about money."

Constantine laughed a little. "Wait, I thought there was only one way to think about money: Make as much of it as possible!"

"Well, while everyone likes to make money, there are quite a few ways to do it! The best way for you to make money might not be the same as what would work for someone with other traits."

Both Constantine and Charlotte nodded in agreement.

"Now you see that shooting for making more is not always better; it's only part of the story. In the traditional economic model of finance, the focus is on four markers. The first is *cash in the bank*, which is easy to understand. The second is *income*, which is how much money you have flowing to you regularly. This can be from a paycheck, an investment, or your mom—it just comes in. The third is *net worth*, or the value of all your assets. These include your cash, car, house, stocks, and the like. It is easy to figure out your net worth! Just put the value of all your assets in one column and all your debts in another. Subtract your debts from your assets, and that is your net worth."

The students leaned in, eager for more.

"You, Constantine," the Professor continued, "have a car worth $4,000, $100 in crypto, and $1,000 in the bank. The great news is that you don't have any debt with your scholarship, so your net worth is $5,100 dollars."

The two students nodded, understanding this example.

"Finally, the fourth is how much *variation*, also known as volatility, that you are willing to accept in the hopes of generating higher returns. Some people are okay with the value of their assets going up and down a lot; other people are not. So, while your cryptos might be heading for the moon, they aren't going there in a straight line. That's why the ride isn't for everyone."

Surprised, Charlotte cut in. "Whoa! Volatility? Isn't that risky?"

"Actually, that's exactly what some people call it," Professor OCEAN confirmed. "Research shows the word 'risk' has a negative connotation[5], which is why I try to avoid using it. Risk isn't always bad. For some people, it's exciting! Plus, it could be a pretty good way to make money in the long term."

Charlotte nodded as the Professor continued.

"While making money is certainly important, what we have recently learned is that how we feel about our money and our money strategy matters a great deal once you have enough money to get food on the table and keep the lights on. We call this *Money Happiness*, which again, I define as feeling that your financial life is going well, not poorly. Simply put, Money Happiness is our overall sense of happiness with our current financial state of affairs. You can build a psychological assessment using the latest psychometric tools (which my Wealth Science lab did), or you can get really close by asking people to rate their happiness with their current financial life on a scale from zero to ten, like I did with Constantine."

"Well, I ain't very 'money happy' right now, so I am sticking with my 4," Constantine piped in.

Professor OCEAN and Charlotte both laughed.

"That will change with time," Professor OCEAN assured him, "but Money Happiness is actually our last lesson. You just finished the first!"

As the Professor stood and began gathering his things, both Charlotte and Constantine sat in silence, contemplating all they'd just learned.

"See you next week for our second lesson!" Professor OCEAN said, turning to leave.

With that, the old man flicked both his and Sigmund's coffee cups perfectly into the center of the trash bin before skipping along with Sigmund in tow.

Constantine turned to Charlotte as they left. "I'm amazed every time he does that!"

Our personality matters for how we think about and how we handle money. Constantine spent time exploring his unique OCEAN personality to improve his performance on the field. Because he'd done the work, he was quickly able to transfer what he knew about himself athletically to what he could learn about himself with money. Charlotte still had work to do to.

How about you? Have read the first installment of Professor OCEAN? Are there skills in others areas of your life that you could quickly transfer to better understand money?

Have you taken the OCEAN profile assessment? If not, we recommend you take a few minutes now to learn about your personality.

Visit us online to get started: www.professor-ocean.com

$

CHAPTER
Three

LESSON TWO:
SAVE IT, LOAN IT, OR OWN IT

Charlotte and Constantine's busy schedules had lined up, a rare occasion that allowed them to walk across the perfectly manicured campus together on an ideal spring morning. All their hard work was paying off, and they enjoyed the time together. After a quick visit with Roy, they picked up their coffees (and Sigmund's pup cup, too!) and headed over to Professor OCEAN's bench. Like clockwork, there sat the old man reading the newspaper with Sigmund by his side. From afar, it actually looked like Sigmund was reading, too.

"Good morning! Right on time," the Professor said, folding his paper.

Charlotte sat Sigmund's treat on the ground, greeting both the Professor and his furry friend. Having taken the OCEAN assessment herself that week, she was eager to share her findings with Professor OCEAN.

"I took the assessment!" Charlotte exclaimed right away.

The Professor sipped his coffee, raising an eyebrow at how quickly Charlotte was getting down to business. She was clearly ready for the lesson to begin.

"Well, it seems like Constantine knows me pretty well. High O, high C, moderately high E, high A, and moderate N."

"I figured," Professor OCEAN told her. "That makes sense to me."

Charlotte couldn't believe the Professor would already have this information in his mind. They'd only just begun to get to know one another, but somehow, the old man had her personality pegged.

"You have to remember, there have been thousands of studies on OCEAN personality so there's a lot of information out there," the Professor explained. "Surprisingly, there's not very much on how it relates to money yet. However, your leadership position on the team offers some clues to most of your personality traits being on the higher side, and the fact that your investments gone wrong bothers you so much points toward high agreeableness and some neuroticism. Again, some studies show that nice people don't enjoy risk."

Here, Constantine broke into a laugh. " I, I must be nice, too, because I'm not enjoying this crypto ride all that much either!"

"Remember, it's not all about one trait," the Professor continued. "It's about the interaction of your traits, experiences, and the story you're telling yourself that makes each of us unique. Your traits offer clues which is all we're really looking for as it relates to money." Here, the Professor paused to sip his coffee. "Now, enough of this psych stuff. Let's get into what you're here for!"

Charlotte and Constantine nodded in agreement, eager for the next lesson to begin.

Our first and last lessons are more

psychological, but the middle three lean heavily on economics," the Professor began. "Any time I head down the economics road, I do extra prep as it's a bit out of my comfort zone."

"I hated economics!" Constantine cried. "Too confusing. All I can remember is supply and demand."

"Well, hopefully this economics lesson will be a bit more enjoyable with a little psych and common sense added," the Professor said with a chuckle. "Plus, the root of all investing is psychological. It's called *delay of gratification*, which is a fancy way of saying that you put off pleasure at the moment for an even greater pleasure in the future. The most famous study on this principle used marshmallows instead of money[6], but it's all the same idea. Wealth is built not by doing something fun with your money immediately, but instead, by putting your money to work so you can do something even better later."

Here, the old man paused before turning to face Constantine.

"In your case, Constantine, you were able to delay gratification long enough to get the car you wanted. That is hard to do psychologically, but it is at the core of Money Happiness."

Constantine nodded, seeming to understand the Professor's point. Charlotte took a big swig of her coffee, eager for the old man to keep going.

"So, if we aren't going to spend our money and we've decided we are going to save it for later, we need to know what to do with it now, which gets us to today's lesson," Professor OCEAN said. "As best I can tell, there are only three general categories of what you can do with money from a delayed gratification perspective: **save it, loan it, or own it.** Try as hard as you like, but I think you'll find that every single thing we can do to delay gratification with money fits into one of these categories."

A little confused, Constantine repeated the Professor's words. "Save it, loan it, or own it?"

"Yes! You can save it somewhere safe with little hope of gain, you can loan it to someone with a high chance you'll be paid back, or you can own something that has a medium chance of going up in value later."

Trying out the phrase for herself, Charlotte

repeated, "Save it, loan it, or own it."

"How's that for an economics lesson you can pay attention to and remember!" Professor OCEAN exclaimed.

"It's definitely memorable and short," Charlotte replied.

"I can certainly remember the phrase, and I'm not bored yet, so that's a good start. But can you be a little more specific, Coach?" Constantine asked.

"Well, let's try a little Q and A. We'll start with saving it. A question: If you aren't going to spend your money, where can you put it?" the Professor asked.

"In my pocket!" Charlotte answered quickly.

"Good answer! And with the athletic prowess the two of you have, that's probably a pretty safe place! I know I'd never dare try to take it from you."

"I'd put it in the bank, Coach," Constantine answered.

"Another good answer. In all their various types of accounts, including checking, savings, money markets, and certificates of deposits (CDs), banks have historically been a safe place to deposit your money because they're what's called FDIC insured."

"FDIC?" Charlotte followed up.

"Federal Deposit Insurance Corporation," the Professor explained, "which is a short way of saying that deposits inside of FDIC member banks are backed up by the US government and taxpayers regardless of what happens to the bank."

Constantine nodded. He'd always seen the sticker on the window of the door at the bank, but he never knew what it meant.

"It gets better," Professor OCEAN continued. "Banks pay you interest—a type of financial rent—for holding and using your money."

"Using my money?" Charlotte asked, not totally following.

"Yes, that's how a bank makes money. They hold your money safe and sound, and you agree to let them lend it to other people. That's how they make money. Historically, in the United States, an average deposit in a bank would earn around 3% interest, or rent payment, from the bank—a sort of financial 'thank you.' The bank would then take that money and loan it to other customers who needed money to buy high-cost items, like cars, homes, or businesses."

"Seems pretty straightforward," Charlotte said.

"Yes, Coach, I think we got the savings part," Constantine said. "That's about all I've done with any of my money in the past. How does the loaning stuff work?"

"Well, like I mentioned, banks loan your savings to other customers who want to buy things they don't currently have the money for," Professor OCEAN explained.

"Like cars, houses, business equipment, and stuff like that?" Charlotte asked.

"Oh, that makes sense," Constantine said, nodding his head as the Professor continued.

"Taking the next mental step, customers on average for all these types of loans have paid around 6%, so the bank makes the difference as their profit after they have paid you your rent."

"Sounds like it's good to be the bank!"

"It's good to be the bank indeed! Still, the bank has costs, like their buildings and employees, so they have to know what they're doing and execute it with excellence. Of course, banks aren't the only ones who make loans. Governments and companies make loans as well. Those loans are called *bonds.*"

The two park bench pupils were intrigued by this. Though they'd heard about bonds before, they'd readily admit they didn't know much about the term itself.

"So, let me get this straight," Charlotte said, "deposits make 3% and loans make 6%? Why would anyone ever want the 3%?"

"Great question!" the Professor praised. "The fancy, one-word answer is *liquidity*, which simply means you can get your money whenever you want it. If you loan a business money and demand it back immediately, it's doubtful they will have it, as they most likely used it to buy new equipment to increase their profits and pay you back over time. That's the *delay* part of the delayed gratification. So, in the bond contract, it states the length of time they have to pay you back. You give up immediate access for the right to make more interest or rent, assuming the business doesn't *default.*"

"Default?" Charlotte asked.

"Another fancy word simply meaning they

don't pay you back! That's why you charge more—or demand more—over and above just putting it in your pocket or in a bank."

"What happens if the business doesn't default and actually pays you back?" Charlotte asked.

"Well, you get your money back and hopefully the business earns a *profit*."

"Profit?" Charlotte asked?

"That leads us to the next category of delayed gratification: own it. After a business pays you back the loan plus interest, the business keeps the money they earned over and above the rent they paid you. And best of all, they get to keep all of these earnings, also known as profits!"

At this, Charlotte perked up again. "I want some of that! How do I get it?"

"By starting your own business or buying part of a business," Professor OCEAN explained.

"Well, I'm not ready to start my own business now. I feel like soccer is my business in a way."

"Good thinking because it is! That's why you just signed an NIL deal. Companies want to associate with you and use your name, image, and likeness to promote their business. It's called marketing. So, yes, Charlotte, you are a business."

Charlotte considered this for a moment before continuing the conversation. "Well, since I have no extra time to actually run a business right now, how do I buy part of a business?"

"A cool thing in our system is you can actually buy a business, or part of a business, passively, which is great for people like you and me. The easiest way to do it is buying shares in a publicly traded company, also known as stock or equity."

Constantine frowned. "My grandpa always said stocks are gambling. They're too risky."

Charlotte chimed in with agreement. "Yeah, doesn't the market crash all of the time? That seems way too dangerous to put my money into."

"Many people feel that way, especially those whose thinking has been heavily influenced by the great depression and the great recession," Professor OCEAN told them. "This thinking—which in some ways is prudent—is why roughly only 50% of Americans own any stock at all. But even depressions and recessions work their way out, and the market recovers to be stronger than before. It happened in the 30's, the 80's, the 2000's, and even in the years after the 2020 COVID crash. Plus, technology has helped with this a lot over the last 50 years. We no longer have to buy one stock; we can buy lots of them, spreading our eggs across a few different baskets I guess. Some people refer to this as *passive income*."

"I always thought of passive income as something like someone paying me rent on a rental house," Charlotte explained.

"Rent certainly can be passive income. But remember, someone always has to fix the broken toilet, which isn't passive at all! Buying a rental property is just another kind of business."

"Okay, I definitely don't want to fix toilets! So, how do I buy lots of stocks if I'm just getting started?"

"There are things called *mutual funds* and *exchange traded funds* (ETFs for short), which are just fancy words for a person buying lots of companies in a type of financial bundle on your behalf. You'll get the good and the bad, but historically, the good outweighs the bad to the tune of around 12% per year."[7]

"That doesn't sound so bad," Constantine said. "12% is better than 6% or 3%!"

"Well, it actually gets better," Professor OCEAN continued. "12% is not the real number. The 200-year average is 6.9% above inflation. That means stocks help keep your purchasing power current with *inflation*."

"What is inflation, Coach?"

"Another great question that we should spend a few minutes on. Before we go on, do you guys have a good handle on save it, own it, and loan it?"

Constantine and Charlotte nodded in unison. "We do!"

Pleased with their progress, the Professor continued with the next part of the lesson.

"Let's talk inflation," he said. "Inflation refers to the fact that the price of things keeps going up, usually around 3% a year but sometimes more. That means the first 3% of return on your investment is really just keeping up with costs. Lots of people buy stocks not to get rich but to keep from falling behind!"

The old man stopped for a second, reaching

down to give Sigmund a quick pat on the head. He eyed his students as he did, making sure they were tracking with him before he went on.

"Of course, when it comes to execution, it's not that simple," Professor OCEAN finally continued, "but it is the high-level framework of how the world of finance works. Grasp those three concepts, and you can make sense out of what the people who enjoy complicating things throw at you."

"So, what should we do with our money?" Constantine asked.

Before answering, the Professor stood, doing his signature flick of the coffee cup into the waste bin. He turned to Sigmund, preparing his pup for their departure.

"Your money's not coming for another few weeks, so no need to rush," he reminded Constantine. "We'll dig a little deeper and explore what all this means next week. We'll even do some mental math—the kind with no phone, no calculator, and no pencil!"

Charlotte laughed. "I may need to have an extra shot of espresso before I get here next week!"

Turning back to his pup, Professor OCEAN said, "Let's go, Siggy! We'll see you both next week!"

And with that, Professor OCEAN skipped away to his next appointment, leaving Charlotte and Constantine chuckling at the old man's disappearing act. Even though they always knew it was coming, the sudden mysteriousness of it seemed to catch them off guard each time.

"Isn't there a leash law on campus?" Charlotte finally asked.

"Yep, but it doesn't apply to Sigmund," Constantine explained. "Word is when Professor OCEAN came back to campus, he wouldn't let them pay him more than $1 per year. He said he wanted his salary directed to a scholarship fund for first generation college students. Supposedly he did have a list of desired perks—some special privileges he wanted in return. No one knows the total list; it's actually kind of fun to guess what they are. I have to guess that Sigmund walking around free was one of them."

Charlotte laughed. She remembered Constantine using a leash to walk Sigmund when he watched the dog. Clearly, the perks only applied to the Professor himself.

"I also know he got a lifetime pass to the college theater where all the new college bands play," Constantine continued. "I've seen him there a time or two."

"What?" Charlotte asked, surprised. "I've never seen him there once!"

"You just have to know where to look, Charlotte."

With that, Constantine and Charlotte shook their heads and headed off to class across the pristinely manicured quad.

Lesson Two:Save It, Loan It,or Own It

Charlotte and Constantine were surprised to learn that there are only three things you can do with money when you want to delay gratification: save it, loan it, or own it! How about you? Do you believe it can really be this simple?

Think through various things you've done with money over your lifetime. Can you put them in one of the three buckets? We bet you can!

$

CHAPTER
Four

LESSON THREE:
THE RULE OF 72

Charlotte stood in line at Roy's coffee shop by herself that next week. Constantine had an early team meeting, so he was going to join her and Professor OCEAN on the bench at 7:00 am sharp. Being so early in the morning, Charlotte and Roy were the only two people in the place.

"Good morning, Roy!" Charlotte greeted her favorite barista as she walked in the door.

"Good morning, Charlotte," Roy replied with a smile. "Money lesson three today with Professor OCEAN?"

"How'd you know it was a money talk?" Charlotte asked, surprised at Roy's spot-on guess as to the content of their park bench lessons.

"I may be quiet, Charlotte, but I've been around this town a long time. I've even sat on the bench a few times myself. Plus, it's pretty easy to keep track of who is meeting with him based on who is in here buying more coffee than they need on his bench days. I also saw him walk past the front window earlier, and the green belt he was wearing was a dead giveaway that you're talking about money!"

Charlotte nodded knowingly, enlightened by Roy's observations.

"Three large shot-in-the-darks and a Sigmund special?" Roy asked finally.

"You got it, Roy!"

Grabbing the contents of her order, Charlotte rounded her corner of the quad just as Constantine rounded the opposite one. In perfect unison they converged on Professor OCEAN and Sigmund. Siggy was laying on the bench, his head in Professor OCEAN's lap while the old man finished up his reading. As Professor OCEAN and Sigmund saw Charlotte and Constantine approaching, they both stood up to greet them. Sigmund even hopped down off the bench to make room for his friends.

"Good morning, you two! Right on time!" the Professor greeted them with a gleam in his eye. "Thanks for the coffee! Ready for some mental math?"

"You bet, Coach," Constantine replied eagerly. "Pour it on us!"

"Before we begin, let's recap. What were the first two lessons?"

"You've got to know your OCEAN personality traits to help you decide how it's best for you individually to save it, own it, or loan it," Constantine responded immediately.

"I couldn't have said it better myself, Constantine!" the Professor encouraged. "Today's lesson adds a third element to the evaluation. While you certainly need to know who you are and understand the categories of money options that you have, you also have to know what the benefits of each of the options are."

"I thought we already covered that," Charlotte cut in. "It's all about risk. Savers have the least risk of losing, owners have the most risk of losing, and loaners are in the middle."

"Great summary, Charlotte!" the Professor said, turning to encourage her as well. "We've only focused on one side of the pain and pleasure equation: pain! We need to also think about the pleasure of investing. That is where the magic mental math model comes in."

"Magic mental math model?" Charlotte repeated.

"Yep! Magic mental math model is a Professor OCEAN original! There aren't too many of those; most of my stuff is borrowed! It beats the academic word for mental math— Numeracy! This one is all mine, and it's about the Rule of 72!"

Sensing the importance of the moment, Constantine leaned in and asked, "Rule of 72?"

"The payment you receive on your savings, loans, or owns determines how long it takes your money wealth to double. Specifically, with money you save, if you earn 3%, it takes 24 years to double; 72 divided by 3 is 24. If you earn 6% on funds you loan, it takes 12 years to double; 72 divided by 6 is 12. And if you earn 12% on equity you own, it takes 6 years to double; 72

divided by 12 is 6."

"That seems like a big difference!" Charlotte observed.

"You're right, Charlotte! And it's bigger than our brains can even comprehend! What we're talking about is *compound interest*, which simply means your money makes some friends, and those money friends make more money friends, and those money friends' money friends make more money friends, and all those friends become your friends! A pretty smart guy said compound interest is the 8th wonder of the world! You young ones don't even know what the first seven are, but that's neither here nor there."

"The pretty smart guy you're referring to was Einstein, correct?" Constantine asked, clearly showing off a little of his knowledge for the Professor.

"Right again!" Professor OCEAN exclaimed. "So, let's put some legs on this. How much was your initial NIL payment?"

"$1,000, Coach. Don't remind me!"

Sensing that the moment for the sting of the lesson had arrived, the Professor paused, waiting a beat before dropping the rest of the truth on his students.

"Let's feel some pain and pleasure, Constantine," he finally said. "If you earn 3% by saving your $1,000, how many years would it take for it double to $2,000?"

Constantine sighed. "I don't know, Coach."

"No, Constantine, you are choosing not to know," the Professor corrected sternly. "Your football job on the offensive line is to block. Don't do it here!"

"In my head?" Constantine implored.

"Close your eyes, Constantine! Imagine writing down the number 72 on a piece of paper. Draw the long division box over the 72. Write the 3 beside it. 3 goes into 7 two times, leaving 12 left over. 3 goes into 12 four times.

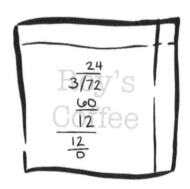

The answer is again 24."

When Constantine opened his eyes, Professor OCEAN was holding a piece of paper. On it, he had written out the division problem to show his students.

"Wow!" Constantine cried. "I think I got it!"

"Great! And what is 6—a rough estimate of bonds over the last 20 years—divided into 72?"

This time Constantine remembered and used his multiplication tables from elementary school. "That's easy: 12!"

"Let's keep going. Referencing the 6.9% above inflation stocks have historically earned, how many times does 12—to use a round number—go into 72? Or, put another way, what is 72 divided by 12?"

"That's easy again: 6!" Charlotte interjected.

At this, the Professor smiled, feeling a sense of accomplishment at his young students' confidence in their newfound ability to understand mental math and how it applied to money.

"Now you can see it!" he encouraged. "If you earn 3% by saving, your money doubles in 24 years. If you earn 6% by loaning, your money doubles in 12 years. And if earn 12% by owning, your money doubles in 6 years. Let's say we're talking about the original $1,000 you received. How old are both of you?"

Charlotte and Constantine replied in unison, "22!"

"Okay, so if you save the money and earn 3%, how old will you be when the money doubles to 2,000?"

"That's easy, Coach," Constantine answered. "46! 22 plus 24 is 46."

"And how much will you have at age 70, meaning after one more double?"

"$4,000," Charlotte answered.

"Great! Let's go faster now. How much will you have at age 70 if you loan it and earn 6%?"

"That's a harder calculation," Charlotte

Age	Amount at 6%
22	$1,000
34	$2,000
46	$4,000
58	$8,000
70	$16,000

admitted while Constantine nodded in agreement.

"Not that much harder. Watch me, focus, and open your mind! At 6%, money doubles in 12 years. That means at 34, you'll have $2,000, and at 46, you will have $4,000. At 58, you'll have $8,000, and at 70, you'll have $16,000."

Professor OCEAN paused and wrote the numbers on another of Roy's napkins to let the information sink into their young brains.

"So, let me get this straight," Constantine began. "I can either have $4,000 or $16,000 at age 70? I'll take the $16,000! I don't care if there's a little uncertainty. It's worth it!"

"And it gets better! Grab your brains because I'm about to explode them!"

Charlotte and Constantine leaned in at the Professor's exclamation. They were on the edge of their seats for what he'd say next.

"If we earn 12% by owning, then at age 28, you'll have $2,000. At 34, you'll have $4,000. At 40, it'll be $8,000. At 46, you'll have $16,000. At 52, you'll have $32,000. At 58, you'll have $64,000. At 64, it'll be $128,000. And at 70, you'll have $256,000."

"Holy smokes!" Charlotte cried. "When you got to $32,000 at age 52, I was thinking that doesn't sound much different than $16,000 at age 70. But $256,000 at age 70? That's a big difference from $16,000! Those last few doubles made a huge impact!"

"So, let me make sure I got this," Constantine cut in. "The difference between my $1,000 turning into $4,000, $16,000, or $256,000 is simply my decision to save it, loan it, or own it?"

"That's it, Constantine," Professor OCEAN told him. "You now know 80% of everything you need to know. The rest is consistency of execution. This is a fun exercise, but it does assume you execute it all for 48 years, which is not easy to do. That leaves a lot of time for you to blow yourself up, financially speaking."

"That sounds kind of like what my coach says," Charlotte said, shifting her voice to imitate her soccer coach. "Charlotte, I'm not interested in what you can do one time; I am interested in what you can do every time!"

"Sounds like your coach is a smart lady!" Professor OCEAN replied with a smile. "Okay, let's bring this lesson in for a landing. A good mental model is for folks your age to shoot for $100,000 by age 30, $1,000,000 by age 50, and $10,000,000 by age 70."

"$10,000,000 dollars by age 70? That's crazy talk!" Constantine cried.

"Is it, Constantine? You might be blocking again! Don't sabotage yourself like many people do. Simply add a zero to our calculations. Didn't you tell me your total NIL deal was for well over $10,000?"

Suddenly, the light bulb went off in Constantine's mind. "You're saying if I earn 12%, I could be worth $2.56 million by age 70 if I do nothing else but simply make some good decisions and execute them consistently over time?"

A grin spread across Professor OCEAN's face. He nodded in approval as Constantine seemed to grasp the lesson.

"Now you're entering the beginning of understanding," Professor OCEAN said. "$100,000 by 30, $1,000,000 by 50, and $10,000,000 by age 70 are all roughly the same number. And not every investment is 50 years away! The purpose of your money could be to buy your first home; which would obviously be in the not-too-distant future. You can use your imagination to move around inside all of your money decisions using the Rule of 72! You can mentally buy and sell things, trying things without the transaction costs! It's a fun ride!"

With that, the Professor stood up, flicked his empty cup into the center of the bin (in a drop the mic sort of way), and turned to Sigmund.

"Let's go, Siggy," Professor OCEAN said to his friend. "Our work here is done for today."

Charlotte and Constantine did not even stand to say goodbye. They just stared off across the quad as the old man and his dog skipped away.

Their brains were going to need a nap.

Lesson Three: The Rule of 72

Constantine and Charlotte had never heard of the magic mental math model, otherwise known as the Rule of 72! They had their doubts that the old Professor could explode their minds. After all, they were about to graduate from college! But, as always, Professor OCEAN delivered!

Be honest, did you know the Rule of 72 before this chapter? If not, welcome to your new reality! If you do know it, do you use it to think through financial decisions involving saving, loaning, and owning? We challenge you to use the Rule of 72 to calculate your version of $100,000 by age 30, $1,000,000 by age 50, and $10,000,000 by age 70.

And, by the way, the numbers may not need to be that high to completely change your life! At a minimum, you can now wow your friends at parties with your newfound skill.

$

CHAPTER

Five

LESSON FOUR: THE 5% RULE

As Charlotte and Constantine walked up to Professor OCEAN's bench the next week, their minds were still blown. They'd had quite the week evaluating both their past and future financial lives through their new lens: the Rule of 72. In some ways, it made the sting of losing their first dollars throb more, but mostly, they were glad to have learned the lesson in a small way while they were still young. They knew today's lesson was supposed to include more mental math, but they had no idea how anything the old Professor might teach them next could top what they'd just learned.

Professor OCEAN seemed to read their minds. By the time they made their way to the old man that morning, he was ready to teach.

Reaching out to receive his and Sigmund's treats from their friends, he jumped right into business.

"I hope you're not thinking I'm going to top last week's lesson," he said with a laugh. "This week will be informative, but last week was the Mike Tyson punch!"

The Professor took a slight pause, sipping his coffee.

"Today's lesson is about the other side of that long-term investment," he continued. "You are young, and if you start investing correctly, at some point you will have a big pool of wealth. You're going to need it! Because as hard working as you both are, eventually you're going to want to slow down, and you will need to replace that missing income. Just like there is a simple rule for accumulating wealth, there is a simple rule for distributing wealth. And that is the topic of today's lesson: the 5% Rule."

"Tighten up your helmet, Charlotte!" Constantine said, turning to his girlfriend. "Here we go with some more mental math!"

"Yep, but this one's pretty simple," Professor OCEAN assured them. "Whatever pool of money you accumulate while you are saving, you should be able to withdraw 5% of that each year and never run out of money, assuming you execute an appropriate investment strategy."

"What do you consider an appropriate strategy?" Charlotte asked.

"Ah, great question, Charlotte! That's a lesson for another time, but let's just say that it will be different for everyone."

"Let me guess: It's based on our personality?"

Professor OCEAN nodded, pleased with his student once again.

"Let me get this straight, Coach," Constantine said. "If I just leave my money in cash and don't make anything, won't my total amount be gone in 20 years?"

"How do you figure?" Charlotte interjected.

"Well, if I spend 5% twenty years in a row, that will equal 100%.

"That's right," Professor OCEAN told him.

"So, if my money doesn't earn anything, I will have spent it all in 20 years and have nothing left?" Charlotte lamented. "That stinks!"

"Yes, it does," the Professor agreed. "It's the worst kind of stench a man of my age can imagine: dying destitute and dependent on my children!"

Charlotte and Constantine zeroed in on Professor OCEAN's face for the first time, realizing he was speaking from experience. He had walked the walk. He knew what he was talking about because he'd lived it. After all, he was only charging them a coffee for his time; he couldn't get by on that alone! Plus, he didn't take a salary from the university. The word was, he was really generous with the community charities he was passionate about, so the funds had to come from somewhere.

"So, what did you do to make it this far, Coach?" Constantine asked.

"Let's just say I had the courage to have more owns than loans," Professor OCEAN explained. "Plus, I kept enough cash around to keep my neuroticism from flaring up."

"That's the N, isn't it?" Charlotte asked.

"My N has calmed down a bit as I've aged, which thankfully happens for most people," Professor OCEAN laughed. "But let's just say I had a little more fire when I was your age!"

"Word around the football building is

Professor O brought the funk back in his day as a player," Constantine said.

"The funk?" Charlotte repeated, clearly confused. "Did you misspeak?"

"My bad! That's just football jargon for being a big hitter or knocking the crap out of someone."

With a hint of pride at the young man's remarks, Professor OCEAN smiled.

"Yep, as you say Constantine, I brought the funk in my playing days! But that emotionality made me a horrible investor early on. You had cryptos, but in my day, it was Telecom stocks. Fortunately, I learned experientially, or as some would say, the hard way. And I've lived a long time, which allowed the Rule of 72 to work for me. Speaking from experience, that last double is awesome! Now, I've consistently spent 5% or less each year, and my wealth is still growing, even at my age."

"That's why you don't take a salary? It's why you meet with kids like us for free?" Constantine asked, clearly curious.

"It's not free, Constantine. I drink a lot of coffee!"

"I'm guessing you've earned more than 5% if your pot of money is still growing," Charlotte pressed the old man. "What did you invest in?"

"On your first point, yes, I've earned more than 5%. And on your second, again my owns were more heavily weighted than my loans."

"I've done these sessions enough to know that if I don't put these lessons together, you are going to ask me a question that melts my mind," Constantine said. "So, let me see if I got this: Using the $100,000 by 30, $1,000,000 by 50, and $10,000,000 by 70 framework, if I grow my money to $100,000, then I can spend $5,000 per year, which is 5%. If I grow my money to $1,000,000, then I can spend $50,000 per year. And if I grow my money to $10,000,000, I can spend $500,000 per year?"

"That's right!" Professor OCEAN affirmed. "I even believe that thinking about it monthly is psychologically more helpful and therefore, more comforting. After all, you'll learn that most bills come due each month, so it's nice to match your income to the time bills or payments are due!"

Here, the old man turned to his other pupil.

"Charlotte, why don't you do that math for us?"

Charlotte's face turned red at the prospect of doing mental math on the spot. She wasn't sure she could pull it off and didn't want to disappoint the Professor.

"It's easy," Professor OCEAN encouraged her. "Just divide the annual income number by 12—the number of months in a year."

Charlotte looked up, almost as if she was drawing out the division on an imaginary dry erase board.

"Okay," she began, "so for the $100,000 net worth, it's $5,000 divided by 12, which is about $400 per month?"

"$416.66 to be exact, but $400 is close enough!" the Professor confirmed. "In fact, it's actually a better way to think about it. Don't get stuck down in the weeds. Go on!"

"Well, I guess if I don't have to do exact math, then $1,000,000 provides $4,000 of monthly income, and $10,000,000 provides $40,000 of monthly income. Wow, that's a massive difference! Why would anyone ever need $40,000 per month?"

The Professor's blue eyes danced as a slight

grin spread across his face. "It sure would allow a person to live generously! And as King Solomon said, 'A wealthy person has lots of friends!'"[8]

"I know that's right," Constantine said. "Or so-called friends who want you to take them to party!"

"Well, Constantine, it's better to be invited and say no than not invited at all!"

Constantine paused, realizing the old man had reframed him again when he least expected it.

"I have to be honest, Professor OCEAN," Charlotte cut in, "when we talk about $10,000,000 dollars, that sounds crazy. My brain kind of turns off, like it's pie-in-the-sky thinking that doesn't apply to me. I mean, I came from a rough neighborhood with a single mom! Who am I to think I could have $10,000,000?"

"Thanks for your honesty, Charlotte," Professor OCEAN said graciously. "Maybe you never get to that place financially, but if you live long enough, you'll certainly have enough skills to help you try! Plus, depending on inflation, who knows what your investments will turn into?

In a way, that's the point! I'm simply attempting to loosen up your mind to be able to think about all possibilities—the good and the bad."

"I can appreciate that. I figured there were layers to what you were doing. So, I think I understand the monthly income thing. What's the rest of the 5% Rule?"

"That's it! Now you know the 5% Rule! And it helps you plan. It gives you the tools to figure out what you need every year to live on and multiply it by 20 to get your long-term retirement goal. For example, if you need $100,000 per year to retire, just multiply that by 20 and find your wealth goal: 20 x 100,000 = $2,000,000."

"That's it?" Constantine asked, surprised. "There has to be more to it than that!"

"Of course there's more to it," Professor OCEAN said, nodding. "I could walk you to meet some of my friends in finance who will run fancy statistical simulations. They might say 4.6% with a wide range of possibilities. I'm a psychologist who wants you to be happy and wealthy when you retire, so I'm keeping it simple and directionally correct at 5%. Plus it makes the mental maths easier and builds your "numeracy" skills. You can get it dialed in with your accountant or CFP in 20 or 30 years. My job is to assist you in building a psychological framework for handling finances. And I think your financial house is getting pretty close to being framed out."

Before the two could ask another question, the Professor stood and beckoned Sigmund to his side. As if on cue, he flicked his coffee cup into the trash and was on his way with a spin.

"I'll see you guys next week for our final lesson," he called out as Sigmund trailed by his side.

Constantine and Charlotte were getting the hang of mental math and understanding its importance. Save it, loan it, and own it and the Rule of 72 are about accumulating wealth. The 5% Rule is about spending and never completely depleting your wealth. Simply spend 5% or less of your total wealth per year and your wealth should last, assuming, of course, a proper investment strategy.

Are your getting comfortable with mental math? What monthly amount would you like to spend at age 70? Are you able to use the 5% Rule to figure out your total number? We'll wait for you while you do your own personal magic mental math…

$

CHAPTER

LESSON FIVE:
MONEY HAPPINESS

When Charlotte and Constantine walked into the coffee shop on the morning of their final lesson, they were surprised to see Professor OCEAN standing alongside Roy. They were struck by how tall the old man appeared with his rod-straight posture. While his face was certainly weathered—likely from more battle scars than they could imagine—his body seemed lean and strong. As always, his clothes were perfect. Plus, that gleam in his ocean blue eyes was timeless, always making him seem young. Sigmund sat dutifully by his side, completing the picture of the Professor that all his students had in mind.

"Good morning, guys!" Roy said, greeting his two customers.

"Looks like you've already got your coffee today, Coach," Constantine said to the Professor. "You still want us to get you another?"

"Of course!" Professor OCEAN replied. "Plus, today's lesson may be a little longer, so I'll need plenty of fuel for the fire."

Constantine and Charlotte gave each other a puzzled glance. They thought most of the heavy lifting was done since the mental math sessions were over.

Sensing their hesitancy, the Professor quickly quipped, "Don't worry! Today should be fun, assuming you know who you are and what you want." With that, Professor OCEAN sped off to his bench with Sigmund, Constantine, and Charlotte in tow. As they walked, Constantine went over Professor OCEAN's questions.

"He's referencing his three questions folks should be able to answer," Constantine explained. "1) Who am I? 2) What do I want? 3) What is my plan for getting it?"

Charlotte took a few sips of coffee and walked quietly as she contemplated her answers to the questions. Sitting down on his favorite bench, Professor OCEAN picked up perfectly where he left off.

"As I told you before we got started, I'm not going to give you financial advice. What I'm attempting to do, without pulling any punches, is help you think about money correctly by teaching you the foundational concepts and reframing a few things for you. The rest is up to you."

"But our first NIL installment is coming in 10 days," Charlotte reminded him. "I was hoping today you were going to tell us what to do with it."

"Your hope is not well founded, Charlotte! If I tell you what to do, then you'll be calling me the next time money comes your way. In that case, I've done nothing but teach you to be dependent on me. Plus, I won't be here forever! Then what are you going to do?"

He paused, letting the reality of his words sink in to his students.

"So, I'm going to give you something better than advice," the Professor finally continued. "I'm going to give you the final lens through which to view money and let you decide for yourself."

Charlotte laughed. "Well, that didn't work out too well with our first payment!"

"Of course it did!" the Professor assured. "You gained valuable experience and learned what you didn't like. And more importantly, you learned what doesn't make you financially happy. How you feel about your money or the decisions you make with your money—that's what's going to be the difference between you being older and wealthy and you being older and constantly stressing over your finances. Besides, the amount of money you have isn't the only thing that matters."

Charlotte and Constantine leaned in at this thought, intrigued at where the Professor was headed.

"Like physical fitness," he continued, "there's an objective side and a subjective side to Money Happiness. You are both in the best physical shape of your lives. My guess is you feel fast and strong, which highly contributes to your overall happiness. Of course, I was once fast and strong, too. Now, not so much! However, I still feel great about my health. It's not based on my 40-yard sprint time or my 225-pound bench press, which are the objective measures. If it was, I wouldn't be very happy with my health! My happiness when it comes to health is age appropriate and subjective. Today, I'm probably as happy with my health as I've ever been, which greatly contributes to my overall happiness."

The Professor paused, taking a beat to pet Sigmund by his side as his students waited for him to continue.

"Money is the same way," he finally went on. "Research shows that how you **feel** about how much money you have contributes more to your overall happiness than the objective measure of how much you actually have.[9] Of course, many people still feel more money will solve their problems."

"Well, it would certainly solve some of my family's problems now," Constantine confessed.

"Of course it would! It would for many people! But back to our first lesson: The two of you are both high Cs and have a real opportunity to build wealth. That's not to mention what you'll make from your athletic prowess. Based on that, it's important that you know about the Easterlin

Paradox!"[10]

"The Easterlin Paradox?" Charlotte repeated. The Professor was always introducing new concepts and terms she'd never heard before.

"Yep, happiness certainly goes up a lot as the amount of money you have initially rises," Professor OCEAN explained, "but past a certain point, it still increases happiness, only a little bit."

"I'm not sure I buy that," Constantine pushed back. "Being broke sucks!"

"Yes, it does, but the research backs me up. You are welcome to learn this lesson the hard way, as many with your personality do!"

"How so?"

"Well, you like to achieve. You like to improve. It's the way you're wired; it's your high C. The world has a way of harnessing these personalities to the plow to produce more. The world can always use more production, and if you aren't careful, it will use you to get it!"

"Is this why lots of the robber barons from the history class I'm taking spent the end of their lives giving away their money?" Charlotte asked.

"Who knows?" the Professor replied. "I'm not a mind reader, but I do know lots of folks my age who get to the top of the ladder and realize that they had their ladder leaned against the wrong wall. It's hard to decide to be an involved parent when your kids are grown and out of the house! In my opinion, that might suck more than being broke, Constantine!"

"Good point," Constantine agreed. "A life chasing the wrong thing does seem like a bummer."

"But money is important. And you guys should make all you can, as long as you earn it by making the world a better place and helping others. Most importantly, you should manage it in such a way that makes you happy based on your unique personality!"

"Any tips on how to do that?" Charlotte asked, eager to hear what the Professor would advise.

"Oh, I'm full of tips, just not financial advice! Putting all the lessons together is where I'd tell you to begin. You've gotten to know your personality and how much saving, loaning, or owning works for you. Your plan for getting what you want comes from knowing what you want and how to calculate the cost of getting it using both the Rule of 72 and the 5% Rule. Then, you should constantly evaluate yourself, what you want, and whether you are actually getting it by simply asking yourself, 'Is this making me money happy?' That's it!"

"That's it?" Charlotte asked in reply.

"Let me make sure I got this," Constantine cut in. "I'm just supposed to ask myself if something makes me money happy before doing it? That seems like asking myself if something would taste good if I ate it! I used to not make my playing weight when I did that."

"Well, what did you do about it?" Professor OCEAN asked.

"What do you mean?"

"Let's unpack the eating thing. You've succeeded in making playing weight so maybe we can use what you learned in one area and apply it to money."

Constantine thought on this for a moment. "Well, the nutrition coach, strength coach, and I decided what my playing weight should be. Then, they told me what to eat and designed workouts for me to get there. I just did what they told me."

"Good," Professor OCEAN replied. "In most areas of your life, you'll need to be your own proverbial nutrition coach and strength coach. It sounds like they helped you measure what weight you were and what weight you wanted to be and then designed a plan for getting it."

Finally, the light bulb went off for Constantine. "Got it! It's the whole, who am I, what do I want, and what's my plan for getting it thing, isn't it?"

"Yup, you got it!" Professor OCEAN said, clearly pleased with the progress. "So, let's apply it to your money. You know who you are. At least on a personality front, you are a highly conscientiousness person who knows sudden losses bother you. Correct?"

"That's right!"

"So, the next question is this: What is the first thing you want to do with the new money coming in?"

Without even thinking, Constantine quickly replied. "Put some in savings so I don't feel broke!"

Professor OCEAN laughed. "Great! Then

what?"

Here, Constantine paused, looking sheepishly at Charlotte. "Well, Charlotte and I have talked about marriage, so I guess I need to start saving for a ring. I'm also going to need some new wheels to get around in."

"Then what?"

"I guess I'd like to start saving for a house. Let's make that two houses: one for me and one for my parents! This is all assuming I get drafted, of course."

"And then what?"

"Then I guess it's time to save for the long term. Kids, college, retirement—the usual stuff."

"There you go! Sounds like you know what you want!"

"That's great and all," Charlotte spoke up, "but where do we put the money? We've got to have some sort of plan, don't we?"

"Indeed, you do," Professor OCEAN agreed. "Ultimately, that's your decision, which will require you to learn and think! A small tip that someone gave me long ago might help you decide: **The price of real assets—whether**

stocks, real estate, and even gold or crypto— is not predictable inside of two years."

"What does that mean?"

"It means if you need your money in two years, don't buy them!"

"The way I'm starting to feel about this thing is I'll keep my ring money and my house down payment money in a safe place—savings so to speak," Constantine replied, thinking out loud as he went. "Then anything I decide is for longer than five years, I'll consider owning something that could go up in value."

"Sounds like a man who knows what he wants and is beginning to have a plan to get it!" Professor OCEAN praised. "You guys have got it! Now, simply ask yourselves periodically how money happy you are, record it, and adjust as needed."

"Record it?" Charlotte pressed.

"Yes! Remember, my simple question is this: **On a scale of 0–10, with 0 being you haven't slept in a month and 10 being you feel the best you have ever felt, how money happy are you right now?** Along with discussing obvious things like your spending plan and account balances, you simply record how money happy you are and refer back to in the same way you'd look at old account balances. Many people think bigger account balances will make them happy, but happiness really is what makes you happy. So, why not focus on that?"

"That makes so much sense! You should have been a financial advisor."

"I'm too old for that," Professor OCEAN laughed. "Plus, that wasn't even a thing until the last few decades. My undergrad Wealth Science class will have to suffice. Still, there are a few good coaches around who buy into this money frame."

"Will you introduce us to one?"

"In due time, Charlotte. One lesson at a time! Remember, when the student is ready, the teacher appears. You guys are fully equipped for the decisions you have to make over the next few months. I do know a good coach can always help. That's why I have one myself."

"You have one?" Constantine asked, clearly surprised the old man in front of him needed any help from anyone. He seemed to have it all together on his own.

"Of course," Professor OCEAN replied. "Plus, one of these days I might start forgetting stuff."

"I doubt that," Charlotte laughed.

Sensing the Professor was preparing to make his exit, she went to ask another question. Sure enough, before the words could leave her mouth, the old professor stood to leave.

"That's it?" Constantine interjected. "I know you want us to think for ourselves, but I feel like I need a little more. We've got a lot of money coming in next week, Coach."

"Don't be afraid to let it sit in your bank account for a while," the old man advised. "Stare at it! That will help you feel your new reality. That's what I did with my first few book advances back in the day. Plus, cash is our happiest asset!"[11]

"Then what?" Charlotte pressed.

Professor OCEAN turned, calling Sigmund to follow by his side. As he made his way across the quad, he turned back to his students on the park bench for one final word in the lesson.

"You'll know," he assured them. "Trust yourselves!"

And with that, the old man was gone. Constantine and Charlotte's precious time with him had come to an end.

Charlotte and Constantine wanted specific money advice from Professor OCEAN. However, he gave them something better. He taught them how to think about what makes them happy as it relates to money and to build their plan from there. Understanding his unique personality, Constantine realized that a fat bank account was where he wanted to start.

How about you? Does the new Money Happiness framework seem helpful to your situation? What adjustments do you need to make in your money plan to make you happy? As you use the framework of Money Happiness, does save it, loan it, or own it make you happiest?

$

CHAPTER

Seven

EPILOGUE

The rest of the semester proved to be exciting for both Charlotte and Constantine. Each of their teams won national championships. On top of that, both were selected in the first round of their respective drafts by teams in Southern California. It was a dream come true for the young couple. One year later, things were still working out just as they'd planned.

Professor OCEAN was on his annual west coast surfing trip when he learned that Charlotte's professional championship game was being played there the same week. Eager to see his students, he used his connections to get in touch with Charlotte and Constantine to see if they would be interested in a coffee. This time, only Constantine was available; Charlotte was playing in the game after all!

Constantine decided to beat the old man at his own game and get to the coffee shop near the pier in their beachfront town super early. He was determined to be the first to arrive. The decision paid off as Constantine saw the old man walking toward him in the distance wearing a wetsuit, carrying a longboard that had to be twice as long as Professor OCEAN was tall, and shockingly, with Sigmund trotting beside him. As Professor OCEAN approached, he spotted the giant athlete sitting in a chair too small with two large cups of coffee.

"Is your surfboard long enough, Coach?" Constantine shouted, waving the old man down.

Sigmund rushed ahead to greet Constantine, disappointed to find there was no pup cup waiting for him on this park bench.

"I'm sorry buddy. I had no idea you'd be here," Constantine said, reaching down to pet his old friend.

"Well, hello, Constantine," Professor OCEAN greeted, slapping his friend on the back. "You know I have to have room on this board in case Sigmund decides to ride."

Constantine shook his head in amazement. "Sigmund surfs, too?"

"Most of the time he just bites at the whitewash, but every now and again, he'll take a ride."

"I may have to see that, Coach!"

Professor OCEAN took the coffee and sat down next to his student. "I'm sorry Charlotte couldn't join us. I heard you guys got engaged. Congratulations!"

"It was the most nervous I've ever been in my life," Constantine recalled. "Fortunately, I closed the deal! Charlotte was sad she couldn't be here, but the captain of the team is in much demand the week of the championship!"

"I totally understand. I'm just glad one of you superstars could work me into your schedule!"

"Well, I've got plenty of time. No playoffs for us this year. We stunk it up, Coach! I know first round picks often go to teams that need the most help, but wow! This one was rough."

"Keep planting seeds, Constantine," the Professor encouraged. "The fruit will come."

"The only fruit my team seemed to grow was lemons," Constantine laughed.

"Well, that means lemonade is on its way!"

Constantine smiled. "You always help me look at the bright side! By the way, how'd you get Sigmund to travel this far?"

"Let's just say that Sigmund only travels first class—another of the perks I negotiated into my contract when I returned to the University."

"Kind of like your lifetime supply of coffee from Roy's?"

Professor OCEAN laughed. "Something like that! And it seems based on those championships, you and Charlotte are in the lifetime free coffee club, too!"

"Yeah, I feel bad for ol' Roy. He might be giving away all his profits with all the free coffee!"

"Oh, don't worry about Roy. He's has had plenty of time on the park bench with me, and now, I'd say he's a 10 out of 10 on Money Happiness. He's living exactly the way he wants to live."

Constantine nodded, pleased at the thought of Roy doing so well. "That's right! I always forget Roy owns a coffee empire."

"Well, maybe not an empire but certainly enough locations to divvy out a whole bunch of championship coffees," Professor OCEAN said. "Speaking of empires, Constantine, what did you decide to do with yours?"

"I never tell all my secrets, but let's just say based on mine and Charlotte's high C scores, we both decided to hold a lot of cash. Then, we set aside some for the wedding and an awesome honeymoon. Once we did that, that ownership thing seemed real attractive based on the Rule of 72, so we got us some of that, too."

"No cryptos?" the Professor teased.

"We bought one," Constantine confessed. "It's a reminder and a just in case."

"And the Money Happiness question?"

"Worked like a charm, Coach. Plus, it didn't hurt that we serendipitously ran into a financial guide who sat on your park bench a few times himself!"

"When the student is ready the teacher appears."

Professor OCEAN smiled sheepishly as he

took a sip of coffee. His wiry silver hair was starting to dry in the California morning sun.

"And guess what, Coach?" Constantine went on.

"What's that?" Professor OCEAN asked.

"I bought my mom and dad a house! A real cute one with a porch and a picket fence. It's not too big. They can walk to town and everything. It's all paid for; no debt at all! And guess what else, Coach?"

"What's that, Constantine?"

"With her signing bonus, Charlotte bought her mom a house, too!"

"Constantine! That's amazing! I am so proud of both of you! You seem really happy."

At this, Constantine beamed. "Yes, Coach, I am happy. You were right! If you get the Money Happiness thing right, it's a big help!"

The Professor smiled knowingly. He was proud of both Constantine and Charlotte for taking in his lessons, thinking for themselves, and applying the tools to their lives in a way that worked for them. Now, here they were, financially happy and ready to set out on the next chapter.

"I do have a question, Coach," Constantine admitted. "If everything about money you laid out for us is simple, why is it still so hard?"

Here, the Professor nodded in understanding. "Of all the questions you've asked Constantine, that might be the biggest one with the longest answer! In short, it seems like our brains are wired to run from bears, not run with the bulls!"

A puzzled look crossed Constantine's face.

"Come see me when your playing days are over, Constantine," the Professor told him. "I might still be looking for new grad students, and we'll have more time to talk about why building wealth is so hard!"

With that, they both took a big swig of coffee and laughed, hopeful about the future and the happiness still to come.

[1]Ng, W., & Diener, E. (2014). What matters to the rich and the poor? Subjective well-being, financial satisfaction, and postmaterialist needs across the world. *Journal of Personality and Social Psychology*, *107*(2), 326–338. https://doi.org/10.1037/a0036856

[2]Exley, J., Doyle, P., Snell, M., Campbell, W K. O.C.E.A.N.: How Does Personality Predict Financial Success? *Journal of Financial Planning*; Denver Vol. 34, Iss. 10, (Oct 2021): 68-86.

[3]Judge, T. A., Livingston, B. A., & Hurst, C. (2012). Do nice guys—and gals—really finish last? the joint effects of sex and agreeableness on income. *Journal of Personality and Social Psychology*, *102*(2), 390–407. https://doi.org/10.1037/a0026021

[4]Murray, N. (2001). *The New Financial Advisor*. N. Murray Co.

[5]Clifton, J. (2022). *Blind spot: The global rise of unhappiness and how leaders missed it*. Gallup Press.

[6]Mischel, W., Shoda, Y., & Rodriguez, M. L. (1989). Delay of gratification in children. *Science*, *244*(4907), 933–938. https://doi.org/10.1126/science.2658056

[7]Siegel, J. J. (2023). *Stocks for the long run the definitive guide to Financial Market Returns & Long-Term Investment Strategies*. McGraw Hill.

[8]Thomas Nelson. (1991). Proverbs 14:20. In *King James Bible*. essay.

[9]Rath, T., & Harter, J. K. (2014). *Wellbeing: The Five essential elements*. Gallup Press.

[10]Easterlin, R. A. (1995). Will raising the incomes of all increase the happiness of all? *Journal of Economic Behavior and Organization*, *27*(1). https://doi.org/10.1016/0167-2681(95)00003-B

[11]Ruberton, P. M., Gladstone, J., & Lyubomirsky, S. (2016). How your bank balance buys happiness: The importance of "cash on hand" to life satisfaction. *Emotion*, *16*(5), 575–580. https://doi.org/10.1037/emo0000184